40 son[g]
for Ch[r]

# The Faber
# Carol Book

Selected and arranged by Gwyn Arch and Ben Parry

SATB and piano

FABER *ff* MUSIC

© 2003 by Faber Music Ltd
First published in 2003 by Faber Music Ltd
3 Queen Square London WC1N 3AU
Music processed by Don Sheppard
Cover by Shireen Nathoo Design
Printed in England by Caligraving Ltd

ISBN 0-571-52127-4

ACKNOWLEDGEMENTS

We would like to thank Sue Alexander, Mike Brewer, Stephen Clark, Hedvig Eriksson,
Howard Goodall, Peter Gritton, Roger Kendal, Ceri Lewis, Lin Marsh, John Parry,
Patrick Rooke, Don Sheppard, Errollyn Wallen and Richard Williams for their
contributions to this collection, and finally Kathryn Oswald and the team at
Faber Music.

G. A. and B. P.

To buy Faber Music publications or to find out about the full range of titles available
please contact your local music retailer or Faber Music sales enquiries:

Faber Music Limited, Burnt Mill, Elizabeth Way, Harlow, CM20 2HX England
Tel: +44 (0)1279 828982    Fax: +44(0)1279 828983
sales@fabermusic.com    fabermusic.com

## PREFACE

Christmas is a time of great joy and celebration. In selecting and arranging this collection, our main aim was to capture an extensive range of moods at Christmas time – from the celebratory to the awe-inspired, the humorous to the more reflective. We've had a great time looking for Christmas material that is, we hope, completely new to you. There are a few of the old favourites, of course, but some of them should surprise too: *Silent Night* in a gospel style, *It came upon a midnight clear* with the American tune or a rap song (*Rapping Paper*) about Christmas presents that it guaranteed to bring the house down! Ten of the carols have been specially composed for this book; we also give the collection a truly international flavour by including carols from fifteen countries – including Sweden, China, Puerto Rico, Botswana, Venezuela and India – without neglecting both medieval and modern settings from all parts of the British Isles.

All the carols are set for mixed voice choir, and most of them are mindful of the limitations of rehearsal time during the Christmas season! This SATB version has come about because of the success and popularity of the original SA(B) collection. The choice of carols is identical (although they are not in the same order nor compatible with the SA(B) versions). We hope that these new arrangements will be used by all kinds of choirs – from small, inexperienced groups to large church choirs and choral societies. Contained within these pages is a source of fresh and contemporary alternatives to enliven carol services and Christmas concerts.

We hope that you have as much fun exploring this repertoire as we have had in compiling it, and that *The Faber Carol Book* becomes an essential and reliable resource for many years to come!

Gwyn Arch and Ben Parry

**Gwyn Arch** is one of the best-known composers and arrangers writing for mixed, upper and male-voice choirs. He has arranged many of the publications within the successful Faber Young Voices series and Choral Programme Series, and is in high demand as a conductor, adjudicator and workshop leader.

**Ben Parry** was a singer and arranger with the *Swingle Singers*. He is Director of Music at the prestigious St Paul's School in London, as well as a highly popular conductor, dynamic workshop leader and vocal coach. Ben has also contributed many arrangements to Faber Music's Choral Programme Series.

## PERFORMANCE NOTES

Many of the songs and carols in this collection lend themselves naturally to the addition of instruments or percussion. We provide several optional instrument parts in the scores, but you might like to explore some of your own ideas: for example, in *O Mary, where is your baby?* you could devise a simple hand-clapping part. In *Moon Dance*, the piano/synthesiser part (the drone) is intended to imitate the sitar (an Asian lute); however, you could substitute a guitar for C and high F, with a cello playing the low F minim to great effect. If you are using the piano, experiment with the sustaining pedal, holding it down for three bars at a time. In *Shiao bao bao* the piano left-hand drone could be played instead by cello(s) and viola if the simple xylophone part is used.

Several of the items have taken traditional songs from countries across the world but have amalgamated translations of the original texts with new words celebrating the theme of Christmas. For example, the original words of the Botswana song, *Tsaba, tsaba!* advise children to take their education seriously otherwise they would run into difficulties in life. In this Christmas adaptation, the lyrics have been turned on their heads, so that it is the children this time addressing the adults and advising them to preserve the true meaning of Christmas. In performing these songs, imagine the context and the style in which they would be sung in their own countries.

Small notes throughout have been used to indicate optional alternatives for the singers.

# CONTENTS

# 1. Starwise

Words: Patrick Rooke

Music: Gwyn Arc[

4

Ti - ny in - fant born to be king.'
Gave them, called Him king of all kings.
Prais - ing Je - sus, born to be

born, born, born to be king.'
for the king of all kings.
Je - sus, born to be

born, born, born to be king.'
for the king of all kings.
Je - sus, born to be

king. Let the song ring!

king. Let the

king. Let the

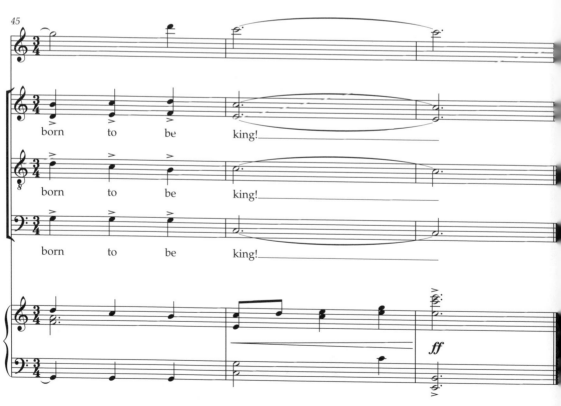

# 2. Sun Carol

Words tr. Ben Parry

Georgian traditional (lullaby)
arr. Ben Parry

* recorder/flute/violin, etc. *ad lib.*

sun,___ please come in._____
sun,___ please come in._____

sun,_ please come in._____
sun,_ please come in._____

Sun in-side,___ sun out-side,_ sun,_come in this room; The

Sun in-side,___ sun out-side, sun,_come in this room; The

# 3. Fum, fum, fum

Words: Patrick Rooke and Gwyn Arch

Spanish traditional
arr. Gwyn Arch

13

# 4. Tàladh Chriosta

## Christ's Lullaby

Words: tr. Ben Parry

Gaelic traditional (lullaby)
arr. Ben Parry

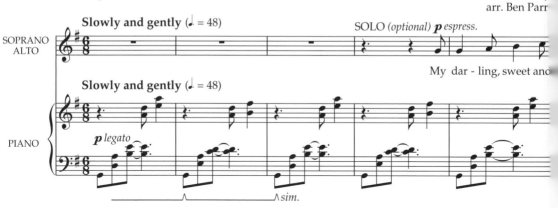

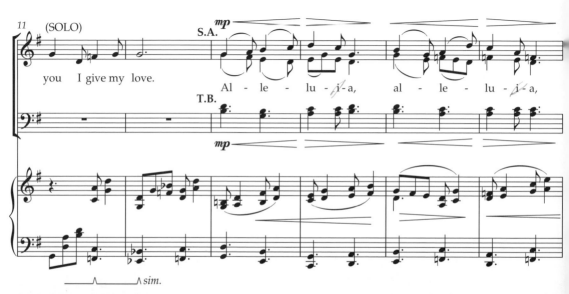

al - le - lu - i - a, al - le-lu - i - a.

**S.A.** SOLO *(optional)* ***p***

My gen - tle one I see you here, my heart so full of love my dear, My

ti - ny, help - less babe - son, you, so full of good, be - yond com-pare.

*come sopra*

20

# 5. Diamond Bright

Words and music: Lin Marsh

**32** *mp* *3*

oo _____ who could ev - er be - lieve it? ___
we re -mem-ber that sto - ry, ___

*mp* *3*

oo _____ who could ev - er be - lieve it? ___
we re -mem-ber that sto - ry, ___

*mp* *3*

who could ev - er be - lieve it? ___
we re-mem-ber that sto - ry, ___

*3*

jour -ney, ___ who could ev - er be - lieve it? ___
ba - by ___ we re-mem-ber that sto - ry, ___

**35** *cresc.* *2nd time to Coda*

We see that low - ly sta - ble,
we see our world with won - der,

*cresc.*

We see that low - ly sta - ble,
we see our world with won - der,

*mf* *cresc.*

We see that low - ly sta - ble and know that we are touched by that same bright
we see our world with won - der and know that we are touched by the an - gel's

*mp* *cresc.*

We see that low - ly sta - ble,
we see our world with won - der,

*2nd time to Coda*

CODA

# 6. Angelus ad Virginem

### The Angel to the Virgin

Words: Patrick Rooke

14th-centur
arr. Gwyn Arc

INSTRUMENTAL INTERLUDE *(optional)*

Recorder, Flute *(8va)*, Oboe *etc. ad lib.*

**CODA**

# 7. It came upon a midnight clear

Words: Edmund H. Sears (1810–76)

American carol, music: Richard S. Willis (1819–19(

arr. Ben Pai

# 8. Moon Dance

Words: Sue Alexander

Indian traditional (Gujara
arr. Gwyn Arch

* Treble recorder/Flute/Violin/Piano/Synthesiser.
† See Performance notes, p.iv.

tap sticks above the head

dance be-neath the ris - ing moon that brings the hap-py news. Come and join us in the cir-cle as the
ce - le-brate our plea-sure in a moon-lit dance of mirth.

si - tar leads us in the mu-sic of the dance. Come and join us in the cir-cle as the

si - tar leads us in the mu-sic of the dance.

MELODY INSTRUMENT

Indian Bells

S.A.

3. Look how the moon smiles

36

shim-mer-ing and bright-ly gleam-ing with her sil-ver light. Watch-ing us as we

tap sticks above the head

Tambour

Drum

leap and spin and cir-cle round the drum in pure de-light. Come and join us in the cir-cle as the

ALL

* MELODY INSTRUMENT

*Repeat many times, getting faster and faster* **Last time**

si - tar leads us in the mu-sic of the dance. Come and mu-sic of the dance!

*Repeat many times, getting faster and faster* **Last time**

# 9. O Mary, where is your baby?

American traditional (spiritual)
arr. Gwyn Arch

* See Performance notes, p.iv.

© Copyright 2003 by Faber Music Ltd.

This music is copyright. Photocopying is ILLEGAL.

# 10.  Christmas is here again

Words: tr. Hedvig Eriksson

Swedish traditional (dance caro
arr. Ben Parr

# 11.  The Wexford Carol

Words: Dr Grattan Flood

Irish traditional
arr. Ben Parry

# 12.  Silent Night

Franz Xaver Gruber (1787–1863)
arr. Gwyn Arc[...]

1. Si - lent night! Ho - ly night!
3. Si - lent night! Ho - ly night!

All___ is calm, all___ is bright.
Son___ of God, love's___ pure light.

Hea-ven - ly _____ hosts _____ sing 'Al - le - lu - ia'.

Christ _____ the sa - viour is _____ born! _____

Christ _____ the _____ sa - viour is born! _____

*D.S.* 𝄋 *al* ⊕ *poi al Coda*

## CODA

birth. _____

birth. _____

**rit.**

# 13. Let me shine

Words and music: Mike Brewe[r]

## 14. What month was Jesus born in?

American traditional (spiritual
arr. Gwyn Arch

# 15. Il est né, le divin enfant

### He is born, the holy child

Words: tr. Ben Parry

French tradition
arr. Ben Parry

*recorder/flute/oboe/violin, etc. *ad lib.*

let's all sing to praise his birth. 1. For a thou-sand years and more, we have heard the
2. What a love-ly child is he! Oh, how gra-cious

he is born, he is born. Ah

pro-phets' sto-ries, for a thou-sand years and more, we have wait-ed, for this time.
and so per-fect! What a love-ly child is he, such a ho-ly, heav'n-ly boy!

ah

He is born, the ho-ly child, play on the o-boes and make a mer-ry noise.

He is born, he is born, he is born, he is born,

He is born, the_ ho - ly child, play on the o - boes and make a mer - ry noise.

*sim.*

He is born, the_ ho - ly child, let's all sing to_ praise his birth.

4. Dear Lord Je - sus, who knows us all,_ still such a ti - ny,_ help - less in - fant;

# 16. A Polish Lullaby

Words: Sue Alexander

Polish traditional
arr. Gwyn Arch

Lyrics:

1. Out of the dark comes a voice soft-ly sing-ing. Sleep and con -
2. Ox - en and ass stand on guard by the door. Sleep lit - tle
3. Shep-herds and sa - ges will come and a - dore you. Peo - ple all

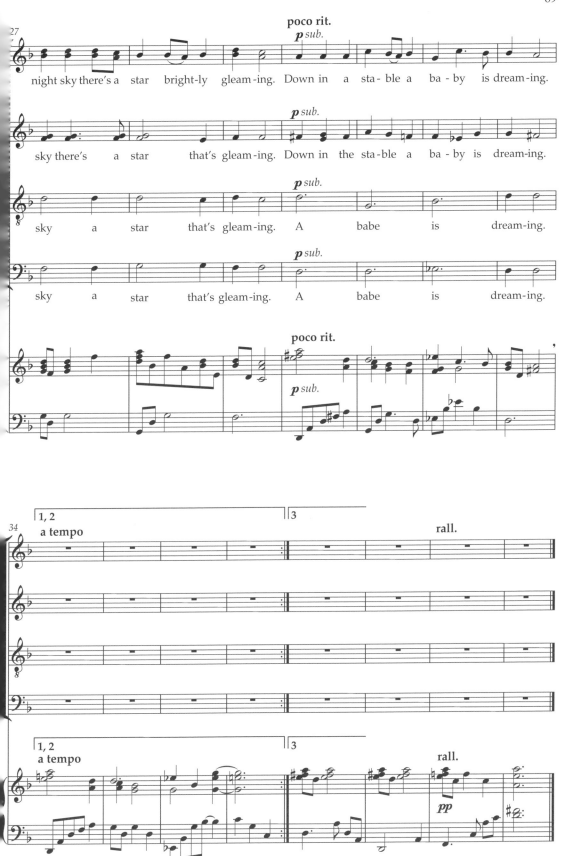

# 17. While shepherds watched their flocks

Thomas Clark (1775–183?)
arr. Gwyn Ar[c]

# 18. When Christ was born

Words: 15th-century

Music: Ben Parry

# 19. The Warmth of Christmas

Words: Roger Kendal

Puerto Rican traditiona
arr. Gwyn Arc

keep - ing. But from that bare stall flows warmth that's deep and last - ing,

keep - ing. But from that bare stall flows warmth that's deep and last - ing___

keep - ing. But from that bare stall flows warmth that's last - ing___

keep - ing. But from that bare stall flows warmth that's last - ing___

with a lov-ing hope to light up all the world. 4. Round the ta-vern fires___

___ and hope to light up all the world. 4. Round the ta-vern fires___

___ and hope to light up all the world.

___ and hope to light up all the world.

# 20. The Coventry Carol

16th-century English carol
arr. Ben Parry

# 21. So many stars

Words and music: Lin Marsh

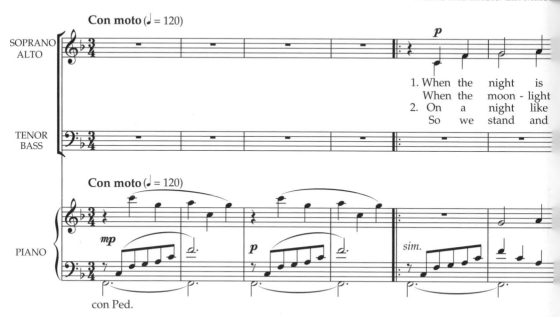

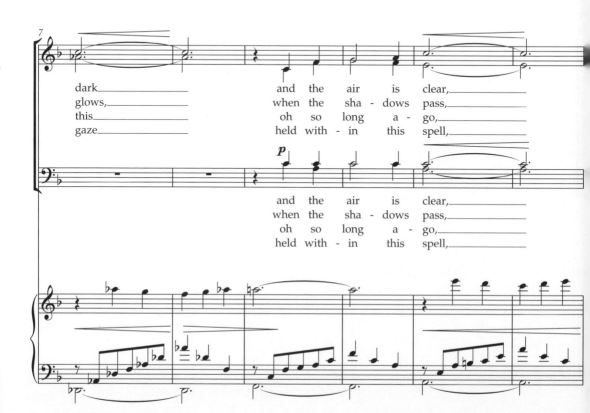

13

Do you look up to the stars in the hea-vens, stop for a mo-ment and
Do you feel some-thing is stir-ring with-in you, stop for a mo-ment to
One spe-cial star led the way to a sta-ble, stopped for a mo-ment, its
Lost in the beau-ty of God's own cre-a-tion, hop-ing one day we'll dis-

Do you look up to the stars in the hea-vens, stop for a mo-ment and
Do you feel some-thing is stir-ring with-in you, stop for a mo-ment to
One spe-cial star led the way to a sta-ble, stopped for a mo-ment, its
Lost in the beau-ty of God's own cre-a-tion, hop-ing one day we'll dis-

19

won-der just why you are here?_____
lis-ten in-stead to your heart?_____
won-der-ful bless-ing to show._____
-co-ver it all: who can tell?_____

won-der just why you are here?_____
lis-ten in-stead to your heart?_____
won-der-ful bless-ing to show._____
-co-ver it all: who can tell?_____

90

*for the people of Trinity United Reformed Church, Wimbledon*

# 22. A Christmas Prayer

Words: Ceri Lewis

Music: Peter Gritton

*Piano accompaniment optional, bars 5–13

94

# 23. Baloo, Lammy

17th-century Scottish traditional
arr. Gwyn Arch

# 24.  Sister Mary had but one child

American traditional (spiritual)
arr. Gwyn Arch

* Breathe anywhere, somewhere in the *middle* of a bar. The optional small notes can be sung by either tenor or bass throughout.

This music is copyright. Photocopying is ILLEGAL.

Jo - seph,_____ and gave him this com - mand:_____ 'A-

-rise ye,_ take your wife_ and child,_ go flee in - to E - gypt's

land._____ For yon - der comes old_ He - rod,_____ a

# 25. Ring, lovely bells

Words: tr. Hedvig Eriksson

Swedish traditiona
arr. Ben Parr

All the fo - rest smiles at us, and we smile back, do not o - ver-turn us on__ our__ jour-ney!
Soon we will be rest - ing by the fire-side glow, when we're there then no-one could be__ hap-pier!

fo - rest smiles and we smile back, do not o - ver-turn us on our jour-ney!
soon__ to rest by the fire - side, when we're there then no-one could be hap-pier!

cresc.

Can I see a__ light that shines from a - far?
All the nor - thern lights are__ fli-ckering in the sky,

Is it home or__ just the__
all the me - mories shine so__

mp

sim.

Sleigh bells

fire__ from a star? Back v2
dim be-fore my eyes:

sim.

mf

f

110

Ring, my love-ly bells, in the eve - ning light! Run, my ra-cing mare, past the moun-tain bright.

Ring, love-ly bells, in the eve -ning light! Run, ra-cing mare, past the moun-tains bright.

Rays of dawn will soon come through the night so black, all the fo - rest smiles at

Rays of through night so black, fo - rest smiles

us, and we smile back, do not o - ver - turn us on our jour - ney!

and we smile back, do not o - ver - turn us on our jour - ney!

# 26.  Tsaba, tsaba!*
## Watch out, watch out!

Words: Peter Gritton

Botswana traditional
arr. Peter Gritton

* *Tsaba, amahy brakes!* = Watch out: put on the brakes! (i.e. 'stop!')

# 27. O, can you not hear?

Words: Ben Parry

English traditional *(Waly waly)*
arr. Ben Parry

Gentle and flowing (♩ = 56)

v.1 SOLO *(optional)*

v.1 Altos tacet

1. O, can you not hear what the an-gels
(2.) sta - ble and see the
(3.) -joice and do not be

*(v.3 only)*

3. Let us re-joice and not be

con Ped.

sing? A hymn of love_____ is the song they_ bring;_____ The shep-herds
child, his mo-ther Ma - ry so meek and_ mild;_____ The wise men_
sad; the birth of Je - sus has made us_ glad;_____ So join our_

sad; the birth of Je-sus has made us glad;

*for Jahneen, Anthony and Tahir Wallen*

# 28. Designer Christmas

Words and music: Errollyn Wallen

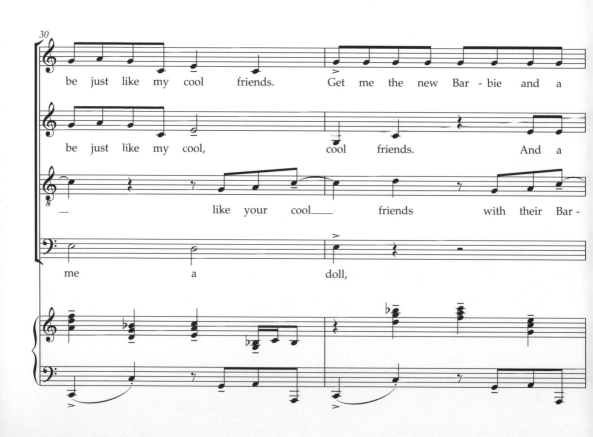

# 29.  Away in a manger

American carol, music: James R. Murray (1841/2–1905)
arr. Gwyn Arch

# 30. Rise up shepherd and foller

American traditional (spiritual)
arr. Ben Parry

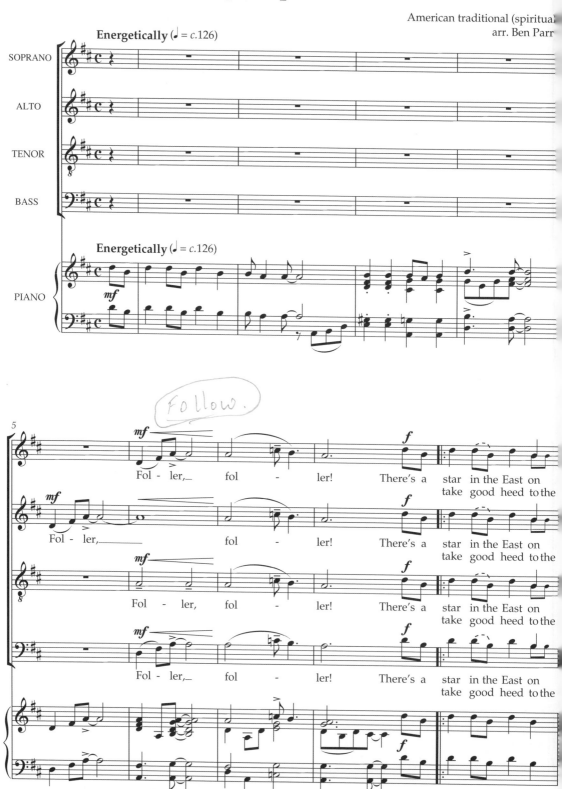

141

# 31. Shiao bao bao

### Little Precious

Words: Patrick Rooke

Chinese traditional (cradle song)
arr. Gwyn Arch

* See Performance notes, p.iv.

# 32. Just a tale

## A song for Christmas

Words: Stephen Clark

Music: Howard Goodall

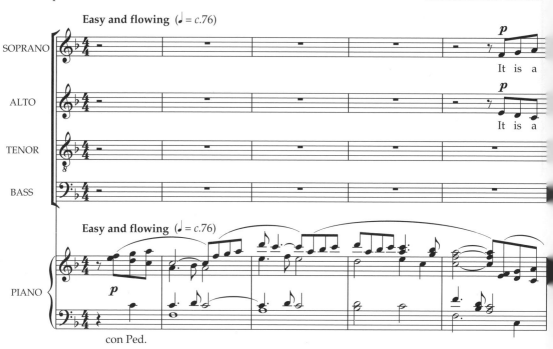

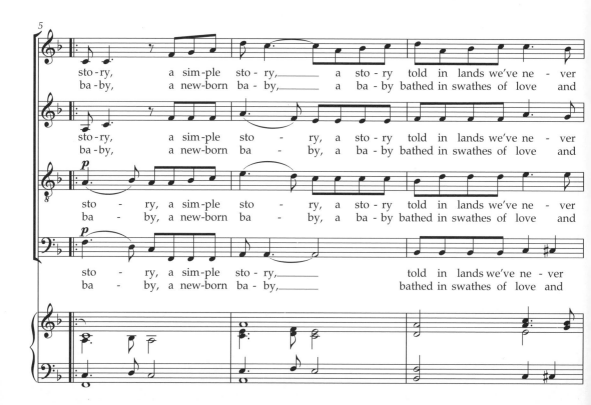

-vives? How of-ten does a wise man die be-cause he dared to

-vives? How of-ten does a wise man die be-cause he dared to

-vives? How of-ten does a wise man die be-cause he dared to

-vives? How of-ten does a wise man die be-cause he dared to

que-stion why we live with fear, and wit-ness lies with tired and soft un-

que-stion why we live with fear, and wit-ness lies with tired and soft un-

que-stion why we live with fear, and wit-ness lies with tired and soft un-

que-stion why we live with fear, and wit-ness lies with tired and soft un-

# 33.  Child of God

American traditional (spiritual)
arr. Ben Parry

*Or hum (mm).

This music is copyright. Photocopying is ILLEGAL.

soft-ly, the Christ child pass-ing, sing-ing soft - ly,— the Christ child born in

- ly, pass - ing, sing - ing, born in

- ly, pass - ing, sing - ing, born in

**S.** glo - ry._____

**A.** glo - ry.
**T.**

**B.** glo - ry.

*p*

*Oo*_____

*p*

*ten.*

*p*

*pp*

*oo*_____

*pp*

*poco rall.*

*poco rall.*

*pp*

\* Or hum (*mm*).

# 34. Cysga di, fy mhlentyn tlws

### Sleep away, my gentle child

Words: Sue Alexander

Welsh traditiona[l]
arr. Gwyn Arc[h]

* Optional instrumental interlude. Oboe/Flute/Violin/Recorder, *etc.* If this isn't used, use 𝄎 repeat.

21

sleep a-way, my gen-tle child, warm and dry in cat-tle stall, rest you 'til the
sleep a-way, my gen-tle child, jew-elled skies be-fit a King who'll rule the world to-

sleep a-way, my gen-tle child, warm and dry in cat-tle stall, rest you 'til the
sleep a-way, my gen-tle child, jew-elled skies be-fit a King who'll rule the world to-

sleep my____ child. Rest you 'til the mor -

my child. Rest you__ 'til the mor -

26

**poco più mosso**
*mf*

mor - row, safe - ly 'til___ the mor - row. Mind not what the
-mor - row, rule the world__ to-mor - row.

mor - row, safe - ly 'til the mor - row.
-mor - row, rule the world to-mor - row.

*mf*

- row, 'til the mor - row. Mind not what the

-row, 'til the mor - row.

**poco più mosso**

*mf*

# 35. La Jornada
## The Journey

Words: Ben Parry

Venezuelan traditional
arr. Ben Parry

what a won - d'rous mar - vel from our God on high.
Jo - seph is her guide_____ as they go their way.
but their God will lead them safe - ly through the night.
Soon they find a cow - shed, so their jour - ney ends.

**CODA**

-reth, from_ Na - za - reth._____

# 36.  Now and then Christmas

Words: Richard Williams

Music: Gwyn Arch

# 37. The Linden Tree Carol

Words: tr. Ben Parry

German traditional
arr. Ben Parry

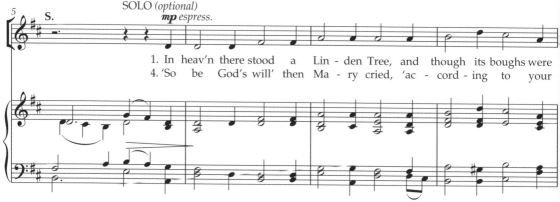

1. In heav'n there stood a Lin - den Tree, and though its boughs were
4. 'So be God's will' then Ma - ry cried, 'ac - cord - ing to your

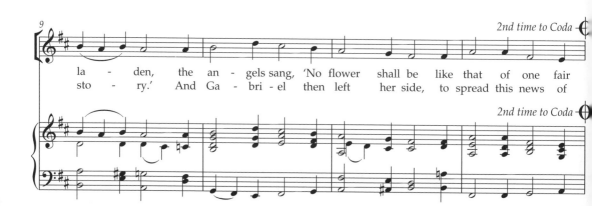

la - den, the an - gels sang, 'No flower shall be like that of one fair
sto - ry.' And Ga - bri - el then left her side, to spread this news of

*2nd time to Coda*

CODA

# 38. A merry Christmas

English traditional
arr. Gwyn Arch

bring to you and your kin. We wish you a ve-ry mer-ry

— to you. We wish you a ve-ry mer-ry

bring to you and your kin. We wish you a mer - ry

bring to you and your kin. We wish you a mer - ry

(Ped.)

Christ - mas and a hap - py— New Year. For— we all like,

Christ - mas and a hap - py— New Year. For— we all like,

Christ - mas and a hap - py— New Year. For— we all like,

Christ - mas and a hap - py— New Year. For— we all like,

bring to you and your kin. We wish you a ve-ry mer-ry

bring to you and your kin. We wish you a ve-ry mer-ry

bring to you and your kin. We wish you a mer - ry

ti - dings_ to you and your kin. We wish you a mer - ry

(Ped.)

Christ - mas and a hap - py_ New Year. And we won't go 'til we

Christ - mas and a hap - py_ New Year. And we won't go 'til we

Christ - mas and a hap - py_ New Year. And we won't go 'til we

Christ - mas and a hap - py_ New Year. And we won't go 'til we

# 39. Rapping Paper

Words and music: Ben Parry

\* The text should be recited loudly and with great energy. Let your hair down!

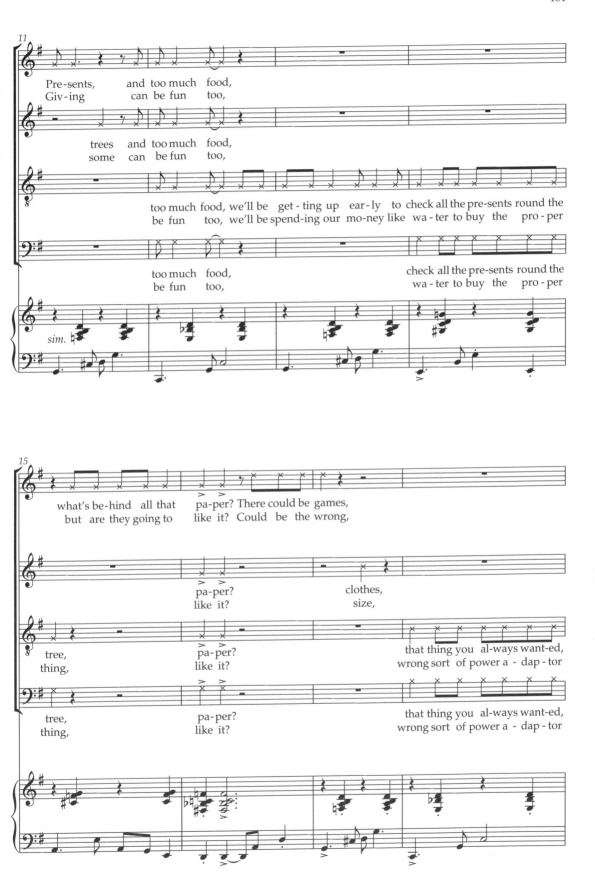

# 40. Gaudete!

## Rejoice!

Words: 14th-century
tr. John Parry

16th-century, *Piae Cantiones*
arr. Ben Parry

*\* Pause last time only, with drum roll.*
*†A prophet of the Old Testament, pronounced E-zee-kee-el!*

# INDEX OF FIRST LINES AND TITLES